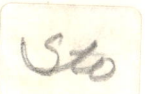

FRIENDS OF ACPL

ABOUT THE BOOK

When Stormy came to live with the Gillis family, he was so tiny that he could be fed only with one of Linda's baby doll bottles. Raising the homeless baby squirrel challenged all the Gillises, especially Happy, their red Setter. How the family and the animals adapted themselves to one another makes a warm, friendly story that comes alive with photographs taken by the author.

Stormy
THE SQUIRREL THAT CAME BACK

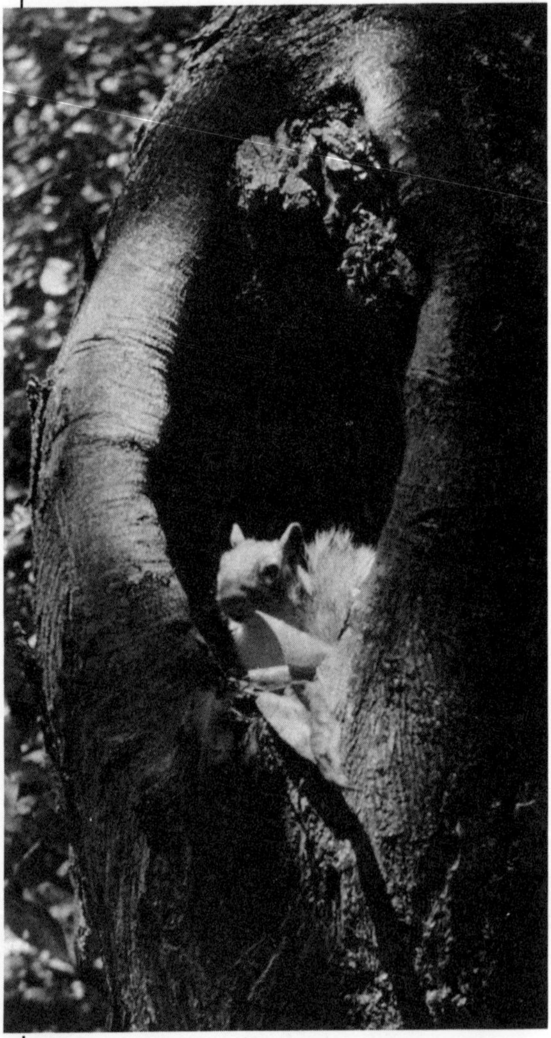

Stormy

THE SQUIRREL THAT CAME BACK

by ELIZABETH LUNT

Harvey House, Inc.
Publishers
Irvington-on-Hudson, N. Y. 10533

BOOK DESIGNED BY JAMES E. BARRY

Copyright © 1972 by Elizabeth Graves Lunt

*All rights reserved, including
the right to reproduce this book
or portions thereof in any form.*

Library of Congress Catalog Card Number 78-93516
Printed in the United States of America

ISBN 0-8178-4682-4 *Trade Edition*

ISBN 0-8178-4681-6 *Library Edition*

In memory of
Norma Kay Neuschafer

Stormy, THE SQUIRREL THAT CAME BACK

$\mathcal{L}$INDA AND JEFF GILLIS waited each year for the exciting sign that told them spring had come. They knew that winter was over when a pair of gray squirrels settled down to keep house in a hollow tree outside Linda's window.

"They're here!" Linda shouted one morning. The shout brought her older brother, Jeff, and her four-year-old twin sisters, Peggy and Emily, racing into her room. In a moment her father and mother and even Happy, the dog, joined the group at Linda's window. All the Gillises liked squirrels.

"It looks as if the greenery in our squirrel apartment is unusually pretty this year," Mrs. Gillis remarked. "I do believe Mrs. Squirrel has a real flair for decorating."

Mrs. Squirrel looked around at the faces peering at her through the window. She seemed proud of her hollow-tree home. Mr. Squirrel sat on a nearby branch and screeched at the group at the window.

The Gillises and Happy watched the squirrels come and go for some time. Happy shook with excitement as she pressed her nose against the glass so that she could see them better.

Linda thought she saw some baby squirrels in the hollow tree, but it was hard to be sure, because

Stormy, THE SQUIRREL THAT CAME BACK

Mrs. Squirrel and the leafy decorations hid most of the hollow. Just in case the squirrels did have extra mouths to feed, the Gillises began to toss peanuts to them out the back door. Sometimes the bright-eyed little animals would come up to the back steps for the peanuts, even though they knew that Happy was watching them through the screen door.

One warm Sunday afternoon Linda was sprawled out on her bed reading a book. Now and then she glanced out the window to check on her furry neighbors. It amazed her to see how easily they could scoot up or down a tree. Going down the tree was easier, because they could turn their back feet and grip the bark. Sometimes they even hung upside down on the trunk as they peered around for food, or sometimes scolded a dog that came too close to their "apartment."

As Linda watched that Sunday afternoon, she began to notice that the branches of the tree were waving wildly in the wind. Even the big limb close to the squirrel apartment swayed back and forth. She could also feel the house shudder, and she heard the windows rattle as gusts of wind whirled against them. Then the sky grew darker. The sun hid behind fast-moving clouds that rolled over and over, as if they were stirred by a giant spoon. Suddenly, Linda saw Mrs. Squirrel scamper up the tree and dive headfirst into the hollow.

Jeff was in his room putting together a model car. He hadn't noticed the changing weather until it grew so dark that it was hard to read the instructions. He glanced out the window.

Stormy, THE SQUIRREL THAT CAME BACK

"Hey, Linda," he exclaimed, "we've got instant night in the middle of the afternoon."

"I know," she replied. "It's kind of scary."

After looking out the window at the boiling clouds, he flicked on his transistor radio. Jeff figured there would be a weather report if a big storm were coming. He was right. An announcer interrupted the program to give a weather bulletin.

"This is a tornado warning," he reported. "Funnel clouds have been sighted west of the city. Take cover and stay tuned for additional news from the weather bureau."

"Wow! Did you hear that, Linda?" Jeff called. "Tell Mother and Dad."

This time Linda did not seem to mind taking orders from her brother, even though he was only one year older. The sound of the approaching storm was beginning to frighten her, so with a final look at the tree, she ran downstairs to find her parents. They were in the garage. When Mr. Gillis heard the news, he hurried out into the driveway, closely followed by Mrs. Gillis. The wind whipped their hair as they looked up at the churning sky.

"It sure looks and feels like tornado weather," he said. "See that low roll cloud, Linda?" He pointed toward the west. "That's the kind that breeds funnel clouds. Come on, let's go down to the basement."

Jeff had already gone to look for the twins. Soon he appeared in the kitchen with his two sleepy sisters. His mother handed him a plate of cookies to take down to the basement. Happy, as usual, trailed after Jeff and Peggy and Emily.

"Do you have your radio, Jeff?" Mrs. Gillis called.

"Right here," Jeff answered, taking his transistor from his shirt pocket and flipping it on as he hurried down the basement steps.

The slightly musty, but cool basement felt good to the family that warm afternoon. Waiting out the storm might be fun, they thought. At least it would be if their house were not swept away by a tornado! Mr. Gillis had built a recreation room in part of the cellar and had filled it with comfortable old furniture. The twins, who were still sleepy, flopped on the sofa. Jeff took a seat near the cookies. Mrs. Gillis relaxed as she sipped the lemonade she had taken down. She held Jeff's radio closer to her ear.

Linda seemed to be very anxious about the squirrel family. "If a tornado hits here, could the squirrels live through it?" she asked.

"I'm almost certain they could," her father replied. "They are well protected inside the trunk of that big tree. Even if it should be battered or pulled out by the roots, I don't think they'd get hurt. Remember, they've dragged plenty of greenery into the hollow. The greenery would make soft cushions that would ease the fall."

A sudden announcement on Jeff's radio made

Stormy, THE SQUIRREL THAT CAME BACK

Mr. Gillis stop talking. "A funnel cloud touched down near here. It happened in open country, so there was no damage."

"Mommy," Emily asked, "if I stayed upstairs with Happy, and if the house blew away with us in it, do you suppose we'd get to the Land of Oz, too, like Dorothy and Toto?"

"I wouldn't want you to take the chance, dear," her mother answered. "Besides, I need Happy. Look at her lick up all those cookie crumbs under Jeff's chair. Honestly, Jeff, do you have to drop so many crumbs? Anyone for cookies had better hurry."

A loud crash of thunder reminded the family of the storm outside. They could hear the rain dash against the high basement windows. A second clap of thunder sent the twins scrambling pell-mell into their mother's lap.

"Boy, that sounded close." Jeff was really scared.

"Too close for me," Linda added.

"I do believe it's hailing," said Mr. Gillis as he stepped over to the window to look out.

"Wow, you're not just kidding!" Jeff exclaimed as he strained to see out. "They're as big as marbles and bouncing all over the yard."

"No new tornadoes have been sighted, according to the latest report," Mrs. Gillis announced, her ear still close to Jeff's radio.

As the thunder and lightning became fainter, the rain and the hail stopped. Finally, the dripping from the trees and the water streaming down the gutters were all that was left of the storm. An "all clear" was announced on the radio.

"I think we can go back upstairs now," Mr. Gillis said. "That was quite a thunderstorm."

Linda raced to her room and looked out at the hollow tree, but she could see no sign of the squirrels. The other children, meanwhile, took plastic bags outdoors to collect hailstones before they melted. Soon Linda wandered outdoors to join her brother and sisters. By this time the sun had come out, and the whole world seemed to sparkle. The air smelled fresh and newly washed. It was cooler, too, than it had been before the rain.

Linda first scanned the treetops in search of her bushy-tailed friends. Then she walked over to the tree by her window. As she glanced down, she noticed something strange on the wet ground near the base of the tree—a wet, brownish-gray object no bigger than a plum. Without any hesitation, she picked it up.

"Mother, Daddy, come quick," she called, but the twins reached her first.

"What is it, Linda? What have you got?" Peggy asked. The hailstones were forgotten.

Then Jeff and Happy appeared, followed by Mr. and Mrs. Gillis. When Mrs. Gillis saw the furry animal with the thin tail in Linda's hand, she gasped, "Is that a mouse, Linda?"

Stormy, THE SQUIRREL THAT CAME BACK

"No," Mr. Gillis answered. "See the beginning of a bushy tail? It's a baby squirrel. Its eyes haven't opened yet."

"Is it alive, Daddy?" Linda asked. She bit her lip, for she was afraid to hear the answer. Mr. Gillis leaned down for a closer look at the object in his daughter's hand.

"Yes, it's breathing. Come, we'd better take it inside the house."

Happy followed the group into the house, wagging her tail, even though no one was paying the least bit of attention to her.

"Let me hold it, please, please, please," the twins begged. Mrs. Gillis took the baby squirrel from Linda and held it so that Peggy and Emily could get a better look at it. But the twins soon lost interest in the tiny squirrel, so Mrs. Gillis handed it back to Linda gently.

"I'll fix a box for it," Jeff offered, "unless you think we ought to put it back in the tree."

"Has anyone checked the tree lately?" Linda's father asked.

"I did, right after the storm, Daddy. I didn't see Mr. or Mrs. Squirrel. Oh, Daddy, it's so cute; let's keep it," Linda begged.

"Sure it is, dear," he replied. "But none of us knows how to take care of a newborn squirrel."

Jeff, meanwhile, had lined a box with soft rags. "This may not be so cozy a nest as the hollow tree, but it'll be better than the damp ground," he announced. "Let's tell some of the kids. They'd like to see what a newborn squirrel looks like."

Stormy, THE SQUIRREL THAT CAME BACK

"Hold on a minute, children," their father broke in. "First, see if anyone is still at home in the apartment." But Happy had already reached the window, and was pressing her wet nose against the glass. She was wagging her tail and her body was shaking with excitement. Sure enough, there was Mrs. Squirrel at the entrance of the hollow. She looked at the family for a moment, then scampered up the tree to Mr. Squirrel, who was watching from a higher limb.

"This baby squirrel has a home to go to," Mr. Gillis continued. "But how am I going to get it back in the nest? It's too far from this window to the tree for me to reach across and drop it back in the nest. If I put a ladder against the tree and climb up to the hollow, I'll scare the squirrels right out of their fur coats. I don't want the squirrel parents to run off and leave us with a whole family to raise. Most gray squirrels, you know, have three, or maybe more, in a litter."

"Daddy, please let's keep this one," Linda pleaded. The tiny squirrel had already wriggled its way into the crook of her neck.

"Well, we'd better check with your mother. No matter what everyone promises, she is always the one who gets stuck with the work."

After the family had gathered in the kitchen, they asked Mrs. Gillis whether they could keep the squirrel. She did not answer immediately, for she was remembering the rabbits and the ducks she already had been responsible for. After that there had been hamsters and then dogs.

Peggy and Emily tugged at their mother's skirt. "Let's keep it . . . oh, please, let's," they begged. Jeff and Linda looked at their mother with anxious eyes. She knew she was outnumbered, so she gave in, but she did lay down some rules.

"If the baby squirrel lives," she began, "it must be understood that we shall set it free as soon as it can take care of itself. This little wild creature shouldn't be cooped up in a place where it can't leap through the treetops."

The four children nodded and promised to accept their mother's terms. Mr. Gillis then telephoned the pet hospital, hoping to find out how to take care of their new responsibility.

"Since this is Sunday, there may not be anyone on duty," he warned the family. While he waited for an answer, the others stood by quietly. They hoped that the veterinarian who always took care of Happy would be on duty.

"Dr. Jarvis?" their father asked, his face brightening. "This is Bill Gillis speaking. I'm glad you checked in at the hospital today, because we have a problem." Then he explained about the new member of the household.

"Yes, I see . . . I understand," was the only part of the conversation the children could hear. He made notes as he listened. The children had difficulty wait-

Stormy, THE SQUIRREL THAT CAME BACK

ing for him to hang up the telephone so that they could question him.

"Hold on a minute and I'll tell you what he said," Mr. Gillis shouted above the noise. "First of all, we must keep the baby squirrel warm. We'll have a number of cool days and many chilly nights before summer comes."

"We could connect a light bulb, then wrap something around it and put it in the box I showed you," Jeff suggested.

Mrs. Gillis recalled that they had an electric heating pad with a cover that was not in use. If it were turned on low, it would be about the right temperature and the right size for the bottom of the box that Jeff had found.

"Now about feeding it," Mr. Gillis continued. "Dr. Jarvis suggested goat's milk, or else a powdered-milk formula that you mix with water. In a week or so we can begin to give it a little baby cereal. At first, it won't be able to eat much at any one time. This means we'll have to feed it every two or three hours. And—it has to be fed that often at night, too."

"Let me keep it in my room at night," Linda said. "I'll wake up and feed it. Really, I will."

"You must be kidding," her brother replied. "Even a bomb wouldn't wake you up. Remember the night there was a fire across the street? Four hook-and-ladder trucks and the chief's car came screaming up our block. It woke everybody in this part of town except you."

"Well, I'm older now, Jeff Gillis," Linda snapped back.

"Let me keep it," Emily begged. "I'll put it on my pillow beside my ear. I'll hear it."

Her mother objected to squirrels on pillows, so the answer was "No!" To settle the argument, Mr. and Mrs. Gillis decided to keep the squirrel in their bedroom. In the meantime it had to be fed.

Mr. Gillis then told Jeff to go to the drugstore to buy the powdered-milk formula. "Maybe you'd better get an eyedropper, too. We'll need something to use in that tiny mouth."

After Jeff had left, Linda had an idea. Why couldn't they use her dolls' baby bottles? She searched in her toy chest and found a handful of small plastic bottles.

"We're supposed to boil the water, then mix in the powdered stuff," Linda said, after she read the instructions on the can Jeff brought back from the store. "It won't take much formula to fill that little stomach. I'll make enough, though, to fill all the bottles. Then we'll have plenty to last until after breakfast tomorrow."

"This was the smallest can they had," Jeff added. "We could use it to feed dozens of baby squirrels for months, and still have some left over."

"If Linda keeps spilling it over the counter, we'll

Stormy, THE SQUIRREL THAT CAME BACK

run out sooner than you think," Mr. Gillis remarked.

"I can't help it, Dad. The openings in these doll bottles are so tiny."

"So is the baby squirrel's mouth, Linda," he replied. "Be sure that the milk isn't too hot. It would be a mean trick to scald the poor little thing the first time we feed it."

Jeff had been holding the squirrel, but he handed it to his sister. Since she had been the one who found it, they all agreed that she would be the first to feed it.

Linda's first efforts to make the squirrel suck on the nipple of the bottle were unsuccessful. Milk dripped on the towel that Linda had on her lap. Some of it got into the squirrel's nose. Finally, the furry baby opened its mouth, and some of the formula dripped into the right place.

"That was a job," Linda exclaimed, as she dried herself, as well as her new baby. In the meantime, Mrs. Gillis took the box up to their bedroom and plugged in the heating pad. A warm nursery was now ready for the young squirrel. Linda carried the baby squirrel upstairs and put it in its new nest. Then she covered it with a soft cloth.

The main topic of conversation at the dinner table that night was what to name the new member of the family. "How about 'Perry?'" Peggy asked.

"Our squirrel might be a she," her father replied. "Better choose a name that will suit either a boy or a girl squirrel."

Stormy, THE SQUIRREL THAT CAME BACK

"Why not 'Mousey,' then," Jeff suggested. "Mother thought it was a mouse at first. It's almost the same size and color."

"That might do," Linda said, "but let's keep on thinking."

Then she snapped her fingers, and her blue eyes lighted up. "I've got it. How about 'Twister,' for the tornado that almost came?"

"No," her brother replied, emphatically. "What actually happened was a thunderstorm. The wind shook the squirrel out of the nest. Why couldn't we call it 'Windy?'"

"Or how about Stormy?" Linda suggested.

"Stormy sounds all right," Jeff replied. The others agreed with Jeff and Linda that Stormy would be a good name.

"Say, Dad," Jeff remarked, "that squirrel will probably turn out to be a girl. Ever since I was born, there have been nothing but girls around here. Linda, Emily, Peggy, and Happy are all girls. So are most of the fish in our aquarium, I bet."

"Speaking of Happy," Mr. Gillis said, "where is she? I haven't seen her around."

"She was under the table a few minutes ago," Jeff replied. "But she isn't here now," he added, after looking beneath the table. "Do you suppose she's upstairs with the squirrel?"

"Oh, no! I hope not," Linda gasped. "Even if

she were just playing with it, she might kill it. Let's go up and see."

Jeff flicked on the light in his parents' room, as it was getting dark. He reached the box first, but when he lifted the cloth that Linda had used as a cover, he could not see any sign of their pet. He even took out the heating pad.

"Stormy isn't in here, Linda," he told his sister. "Quick, let's look under the beds." The children began to search every inch of the room, but they could not find Stormy.

"What could have happened?" Linda cried. "Where is Happy? What could she have done with poor little Stormy? I'm too scared to find out."

Just then Happy appeared. She wagged her tail as she went from one of the family to the other, expecting a pat and a greeting. Instead of a pat, she received a scolding. "What did you do to that squirrel, you stupid dog?" Jeff said.

"Bad, bad Happy," Peggy added.

"How could you do it, Happy?" Linda cried, as she fought back the tears.

Happy's tail stopped wagging and disappeared between her back legs. Her reddish-gold head lowered as she looked up with questioning brown eyes. She didn't know why she was in disgrace.

"Let the dog alone," Mr. Gillis said. "She doesn't understand what this is all about."

"I have a thought," said her husband, cheer-

Stormy, THE SQUIRREL THAT CAME BACK

fully. "Happy sometimes hides my socks in the living room. Why don't we look around there? Come on, Linda," he said, as he put his arm around his daughter's shoulders. "Don't give up. Stormy has to be somewhere in the house."

He got down on all fours and peered under the sofa. He looked on top of the cushions. He lifted a pillow. There, curled in a ball, lay the squirrel.

"Here's Stormy," he called. "Here's where Happy put it." As the others crowded around him, he picked up the baby squirrel. "Nothing wrong with this little baby. It was taking a nap, that's all. Squirrels sure sleep soundly."

"Oh, Stormy, I'm so glad to see you," Linda cried. "Forgive me, Happy," she added, as she turned to welcome the dog, who came up to her, tail wagging again. "I should have known that a nice, gentle dog like you would never harm this little helpless thing." Linda hugged Happy, and the dog, in turn, licked Linda's face.

"I'm as limp as a wet noodle," Mrs. Gillis remarked. "We do not need to worry any more about Happy hurting the squirrel. But for safety's sake, let's keep the bedroom door closed when Stormy is in there alone."

"I think Stormy brought out the mother instinct in Happy," her husband remarked. "Since she's never had any pups, she may have decided to substitute a squirrel for a puppy."

At bedtime that night Jeff and the twins took turns feeding Stormy. Milk was splattered everywhere in the process, but some evidently did get down Stormy's throat. At least, the squirrel seemed content to curl up in its box for another nap.

After reminding their parents to set the alarm clock for the next feeding, the children headed for their rooms and beds.

Around the breakfast table the next morning Mr. and Mrs. Gillis reported that everything had gone well during the night.

"We took turns," their mother said. "I've had better nights of sleep, however. Even though I knew your father was going to take the next feeding, I listened for the alarm to ring."

During breakfast, Happy sat in her favorite chair by the window. Linda moved her chair over close to the dog, for she wanted Happy to know she loved her, despite the scolding she had given the dog the night before. Happy showed her pleasure by wagging her tail, but she continued to look out the window for squirrels or dogs in the yard.

"Little creatures grow very fast," Mr. Gillis reminded his wife, as they sipped their coffee. "It shouldn't be long before Stormy will eat enough to get through the night without having to be fed."

※　※　※　※　※

Just as everyone thought Stormy was well on her way to bigger meals, she stopped eating. What

Stormy, THE SQUIRREL THAT CAME BACK

was worse, she seemed to be puffed up and swollen.

"What do you think is wrong?" Linda asked her mother.

"I don't know, dear. Maybe I'd better call Dr. Jarvis right away."

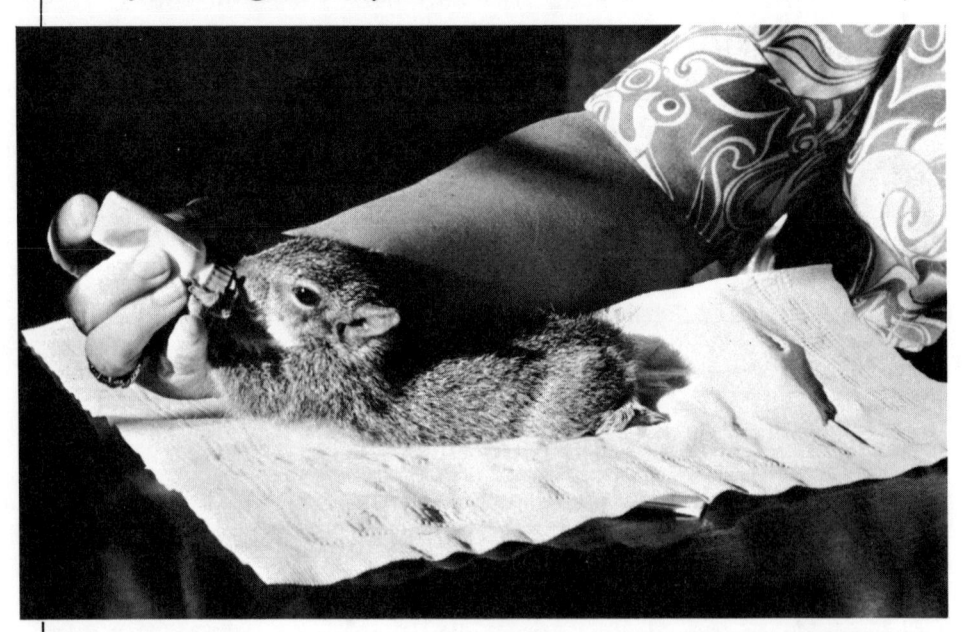

"Oh, please do, Mother. We can't let anything happen to Stormy now. She has already become one of the family."

After the doctor had heard about Stormy's troubles, he explained that a mother squirrel "bathes" her babies after each feeding by licking them. The moist, licking motion helps the baby to digest its food. He suggested that the Gillises try to imitate this idea by bathing Stormy in warm, swirling water.

"My goodness, I've never bathed anything this

small before," Mrs. Gillis laughed, as she and Linda took Stormy to the bathroom.

"Mother, please don't put too much water in the bowl."

"Don't worry, Linda," she replied. "I won't even close the drain. I hope the running water and the movement of my finger tips will help Stormy's digestion. I'll bet she's miserable."

For two days Mrs. Gillis bathed the baby squirrel after each feeding. No one played with Stormy while it was sick. When the neighborhood children came to the door to see the squirrel, they were told to come back another day.

After each bath Linda dried the wet fur with a cloth. She noticed that the fuzz on Stormy's tail did not stand out when it was wet, so Linda could understand why her mother had thought that Stormy was a mouse. Squirrels were cuter dry.

Just as suddenly as it had been taken sick, Stormy was well and opened her bright eyes for the first time. As Jeff had predicted, the family decided that Stormy was a girl squirrel. Her movements gave a hint of the grace and quickness of the adult squirrel she would soon become.

When the children took Stormy out of the box, she scampered up and down their bodies, as if they were tree trunks. She still loved to burrow in the warmth of their necks.

Mr. and Mrs. Gillis never had any trouble get-

Stormy, THE SQUIRREL THAT CAME BACK

ting baby sitters when they wanted to go out, after Stormy joined the family. Lucy, a teenager whom the children liked the best, even came when she wasn't needed. Stormy loved to hide in her long hair. It wasn't easy for Lucy to pull the squirrel out of her tangled hair, but she didn't seem to mind. Stormy's sharp claws clung to Lucy's hair as she burrowed deeper under her collar.

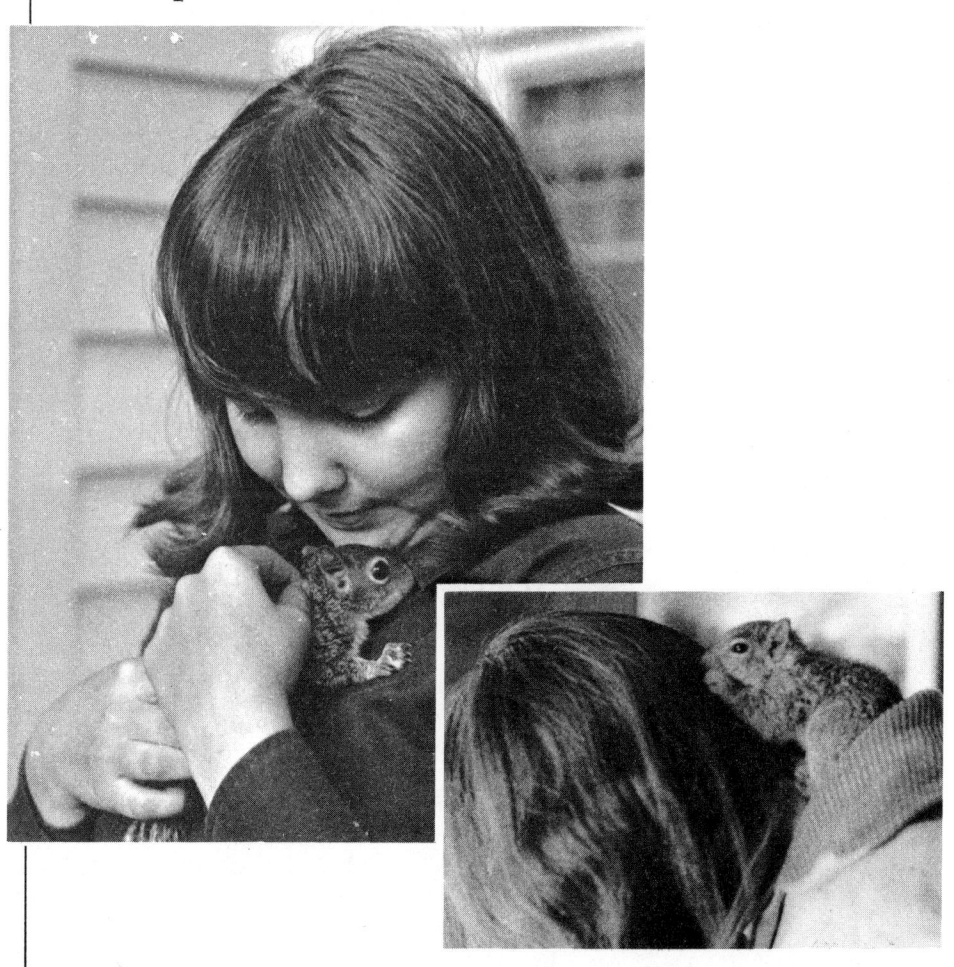

"Brother, you would really be mad if one of us messed up your precious hair like that," Jeff told Lucy.

Stormy, THE SQUIRREL THAT CAME BACK

"You are right, Jeff Gillis, so don't ever try it. But Stormy can tangle my hair anytime," Lucy added, grabbing hold of the little squirrel before she disappeared down the back of Lucy's jacket.

"Lucy loves Stormy more than she does us," Emily cried, with a note of jealousy in her voice.

"Oh, I wouldn't say that, Emily," Lucy replied, as she lifted the little girl onto her lap and handed her the bright-eyed squirrel."

* * * * *

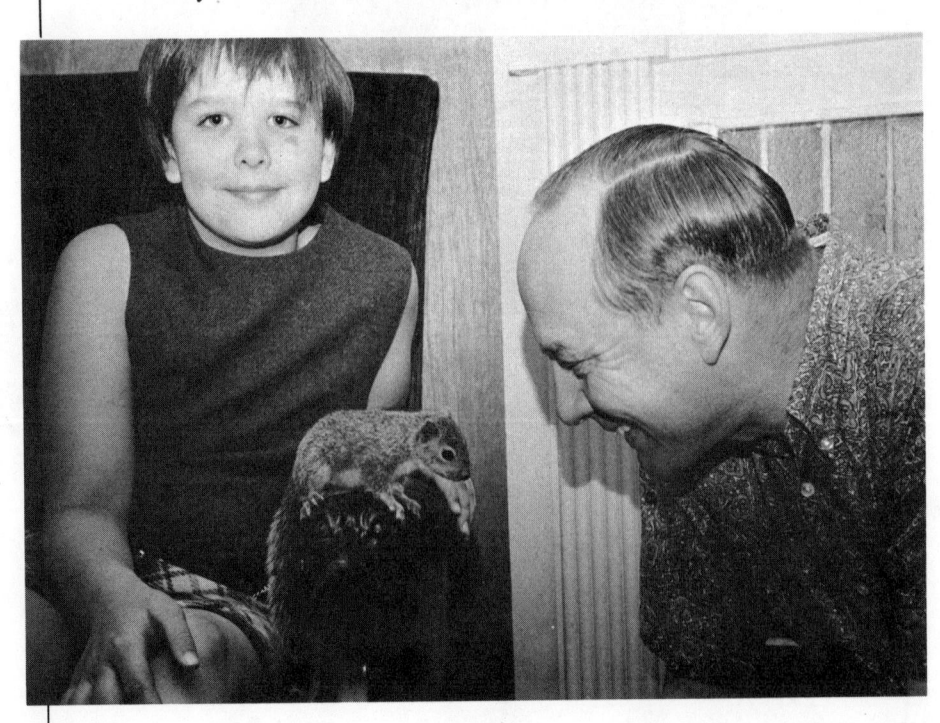

The fuzzy tail that Stormy had sucked on, just as a baby sometimes sucks its thumb, soon grew bushy. She liked to flick it and swish it around. She also used it to keep her balance. After she had been with the family for three weeks, Stormy could get out of her box with a jump and a swish of her tail. When Mr. Gillis came home from work one afternoon and found a small squirrel turning summersaults on his favorite chair . . . well, everyone thought he'd be angry. Instead, he seemed to enjoy Stormy's playfulness. No one could get mad at Stormy.

"Stormy gets cuter-looking all the time," Linda told her brother. "She's such fun. My pendant watch attracts her. She doesn't know what to make of it."

"I'd rather she'd chew on that thing than on my finger," Jeff remarked. "I think, though, she's lost most of her baby teeth by now. Anyway, whatever she has in her mouth is plenty sharp."

33

Stormy, THE SQUIRREL THAT CAME BACK

Feeding Stormy soon became easier than it had been at the beginning. She took cereal from an eyedropper in addition to the formula from the doll bottle. Neither were there so many night feedings. Mr.

and Mrs. Gillis no longer needed to set the alarm clock, for Stormy scratched on the side of the box to let them know when she was hungry.

The scratching was about the only sound Stormy made until one afternoon after Linda had fed her.

"I heard silly little noises," Linda told her mother. "I looked all around trying to figure out what the noise was. Then I knew. Stormy had the hiccups!"

✿ ✿ ✿ ✿ ✿

As the weather grew warmer and as Stormy outgrew her box, the Gillises had to find another house for her. They decided that the screened-in porch would be the best place. It would provide plenty of fresh air and also room to leap around. Besides, there wasn't much damage a squirrel could do out there.

When the family moved Stormy to the porch, Mrs. Gillis reminded the children that the screened door leading from the porch to the back yard must not only be closed but also locked at all times.

"One careless moment," she warned, "and Stormy could be killed. There are dogs in the neighborhood that are not so gentle as Happy. Besides, the cats roaming around here are more of a danger than the dogs."

When Stormy became a porch dweller, she also changed her eating habits and began to enjoy sunflower seeds and nuts that the family brought her.

Stormy, THE SQUIRREL THAT CAME BACK

When Jeff was sure that no dogs or cats were around, he took her out in the yard to play in the grass. He watched over her as she hopped among the tall green blades, stopping now and then to dig in the ground or to scratch herself. When he wanted her to come to him, he held out an acorn. After Stormy took the nut from Jeff's fingers with her teeth, she jumped up to his shoulder and perched next to his ear. Then she turned the nut around and around in her front paws as she removed the shell. If Jeff gave her a peanut,

Stormy, THE SQUIRREL THAT CAME BACK

Stormy removed the reddish husk as well as the shell before eating the nut.

The bigger Stormy became, the more she littered up the porch with shells, husks from sunflower seeds, and torn-up paper. The litter piled up with discouraging speed, and of course it was Mrs. Gillis who had to do most of the cleaning. The children always could find excuses. Jeff had baseball practice, Scout meetings, homework, and guitar lessons. Linda was busy with Girl Scouts, piano practice, and her girls' softball team. Besides, she always had a way of disappearing on her bicycle when she was needed.

One day Mrs. Gillis decided that the weather was warm enough to put out the porch furniture that had been stored in the garage. Perhaps if she hosed it and then touched up the bad spots with a little paint, the whole family could enjoy the porch. That is, they could if Stormy were put somewhere else. But where?

Mrs. Gillis knew how upset the children would be if she should set Stormy free. But she thought that the sooner everyone faced that problem, the better. At dinner that night she reminded the family of the promise they had made the night after the storm.

"I've noticed other young squirrels running loose in the yard," she said. "Some of those may be from the same litter as Stormy. We have raised a sleek, healthy squirrel. The way she leaps around that porch I know she'll make herself right at home."

The children never spoke. Linda bit her lip, and Jeff stared at his plate. Peggy and Emily sat wide-eyed and silent.

After taking a deep breath, Mrs. Gillis continued. "Tomorrow morning we'll free Stormy. Sorry, my dears, but your father and I have talked this over, and this is the way it has to be."

"We need our porch to sit on this summer," Mr. Gillis added. "Besides, we all know that a squirrel shouldn't spend its life indoors. Come on. Cheer up, children, and finish your dinner."

"But what about the cat across the street?" Jeff asked plaintively. "And the Johnsons' dog. We know he's killed a squirrel."

39

Stormy, THE SQUIRREL THAT CAME BACK

"Remember your promise, Jeff," his father replied, so Jeff nodded and said nothing further.

That evening the house was much quieter than usual. Although nobody said anything, everyone was thinking about Stormy. Jeff made a half-hearted try at playing ball with Happy. Even the dog seemed to know that something had changed. After fetching the ball a couple of times, she let it drop from her mouth, then wandered off to a corner to lie down.

The family's spirits weren't much better at breakfast the next morning. After they had finished eating, Mr. Gillis told Jeff to check to see whether there were any dogs or cats around. Then he put his arm around Linda. He asked her to get Stormy and to bring her out to the back yard.

Happy was the only one to remain inside as the family gathered to free their pet. It was a beautiful morning, so the sunshine helped somewhat to make everyone feel better and not quite so sad.

But when Stormy was put down in the yard, she didn't seem to know what to do. She was in no hurry to go anywhere.

"We sure must look stupid," Jeff remarked. "Here we are, all standing around watching that silly squirrel. Go on, Stormy, or I'll be late for school."

"I see one of your friends," Peggy said, as she suddenly spied a squirrel hopping across the garage roof. Even this idea didn't impress Stormy, who was sitting down in the grass scratching herself.

Just as Linda and Jeff decided it was about time to leave for school, or else be tardy, Stormy took a few long hops. She jumped to the trunk of a tree and began to climb part way up. There she stopped and looked back at her family. Then, with a flick of her tail she climbed higher up the trunk.

Craning their necks, the Gillises watched as the squirrel raced along a branch over their heads. To

Stormy, THE SQUIRREL THAT CAME BACK

their amazement she began to jump from one branch to another. Stormy's leaps looked more like flying to Linda.

"On your way, gang," their father ordered. "Summer vacation is almost here. When school is out, you can watch squirrels all you want to."

In the following weeks the children did see Stormy from time to time. Once she took a peanut from Jeff. Then she hopped on his shoulder to eat it, as she had done before, but when he tried to hold her, she darted off out of reach.

It was hard to tell Stormy from the other squirrels in the trees. Up close, the children knew their pet, because she was friendlier and less afraid. The first member of the family that came to the kitchen in the morning would open the back door to find Stormy waiting on the top step. If no one opened the door, the squirrel would climb up on the screen door and make a terrible racket. Sometimes she would perch in a nearby tree and screech until the family heard her and tossed out some peanuts.

Now that Stormy was grown and free, Happy chased her just as she did all the other squirrels. As always, the dog came in second. To make matters worse for poor Happy, Stormy often scooted down the tree trunk far enough for the dog to reach her. Happy would then race to the tree, and just as she was ready to jump, Stormy would dodge to one side or the other. Time and again the dog would leap at

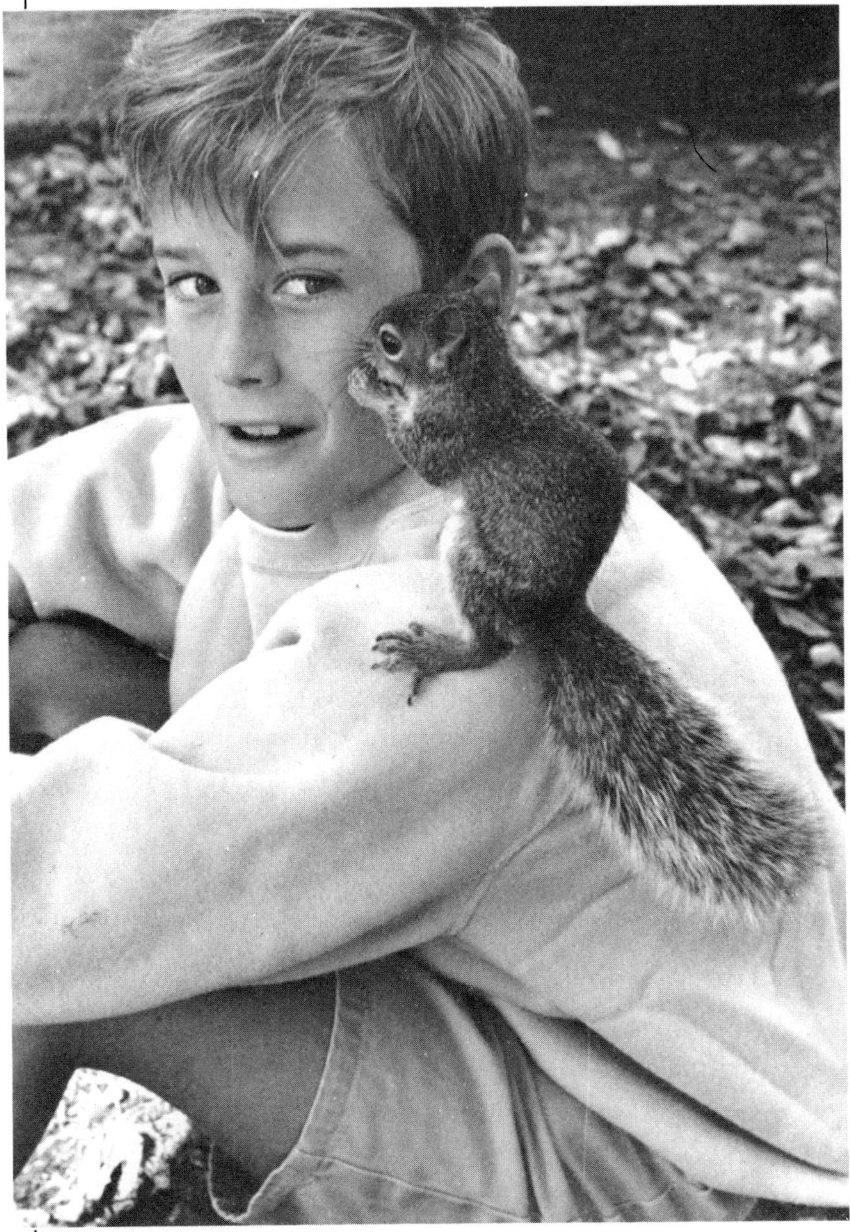

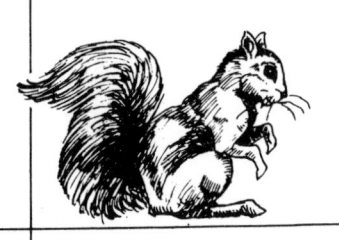

Stormy, THE SQUIRREL THAT CAME BACK

the tree while the squirrel would go round and round the trunk. Happy never seemed to tire of this teasing. It was a game both animals enjoyed. The Gillises also enjoyed watching them, usually from the breakfast-room windows.

A day came when Stormy was not to be seen. She wasn't at the back door; nor was she scolding from the tree branches. Happy waited in vain for her playmate.

"Do you suppose something has happened to her?" Linda asked her brother.

"I sure hope not," Jeff replied. "Don't tell the others, but I heard today from some of the boys down

Stormy, THE SQUIRREL THAT CAME BACK

the street that the Johnsons' dog had just killed another squirrel. Of course the boys didn't know whether it was Stormy."

"Oh, Jeff," Linda cried, "why did you have to tell me that? Now I'm really worried." The two agreed not to say anything about it to the twins or to their parents.

It wasn't as much fun after that to sit at the breakfast-room table and not be able to see Happy and Stormy playing hide-and-seek around the trees. They did see other squirrels, however, and also some beautiful red cardinals. Seeing the colorful birds gave Mr. Gillis an idea.

The following afternoon when he came home from work, he told the family that he had brought them a surprise. The twins began to guess, but their father said they might as well give up, as none of them could figure it out in a million years.

While he opened the car trunk, the whole family gathered around. Jeff reached in to pull out a large carton.

"Oh, boy, it's pretty big," Emily exclaimed.

Jeff held the box while his father took out a wooden piece with a glass top that looked like a shelf, only it was different.

"What is it?" Linda asked.

"Wait and see," her father replied. "Please get a screwdriver, then I'll show you."

Carrying the bulky thing under his arm, he

47

Stormy, THE SQUIRREL THAT CAME BACK

walked around to the back of the house and stopped at Happy's favorite window. When Linda handed him the screwdriver, he told Jeff that he also needed a drill to make a couple of holes.

"I'll get it," Jeff said. "I bet this thing screws onto the windowsill, but what's it for?"

"You'll soon find out," his father replied, smiling, as he placed it against the wall.

Father and son worked together, and soon they had the shelf in place.

"Now, my dear," Mr. Gillis said to his wife, "if you'll find the sunflower seeds, we'll be in business. Squirrels aren't the only one who like sunflower seeds. Cardinals love them. In a few days we should be able to lure Mr. and Mrs. Cardinal right up to this window. It ought to be exciting to watch them."

"So it's a bird feeder!" Linda exclaimed. "That's a neat idea, Dad."

As the family sat at breakfast the next morning, they kept a sharp lookout for the cardinals. Happy sat at her usual post at the window.

"It may take the birds a while to get used to Happy staring out at them," Mrs. Gillis remarked.

"Speaking of Happy," Jeff said, "what's her problem? Look, she's shaking like a leaf."

At that instant Happy jumped. So did everyone else. On the feeder peering in at them was a gray squirrel! Stormy had come back! After she had looked everyone over, she whirled around and ducked inside the feeder where she stuffed herself with sunflower seeds. The tiny jaws went at full speed, hulls scattering in every direction.

"Looks as if the cardinals will have to wait in line," Linda said, laughing. Stormy came to the window after she had had her fill, and peered in the room. All that separated her from Happy was a pane of glass.

Linda slowly opened the window a few inches and poked her hand out, a peanut between her fingers. Stormy snatched the nut, then jumped to the ground. The family watched her as she buried it in the yard, then hopped back to the feeder for more. Each of the children took turns feeding Stormy, while Happy quivered with excitement as she looked out the window.

Stormy, THE SQUIRREL THAT CAME BACK

After that, visits at the window with Stormy took place daily. Usually, she showed up several times a day. If the window were partly open, the

50

children put nuts just inside it on the sill. The squirrel would then stick her paw inside to snatch them away from under Happy's nose.

Stormy, THE SQUIRREL THAT CAME BACK

53

Stormy, THE SQUIRREL THAT CAME BACK

"Remember, Stormy is a wild creature by this time," Mr. Gillis reminded the family. "Don't let her into the house. She would become frightened and hurt herself, or maybe bite one of us or chew up something."

The children didn't lure the squirrel any further than the windowsill. Now and then, however, they did forget to close the window. When that happened, Stormy "sneaked" inside. One day she discovered a can full of peanuts on the table. Mrs. Gillis found her, headfirst in the can, helping herself.

"You little housebreaker, scat!" The squirrel ducked back through the open window, a peanut in her mouth. At other times Stormy's secret visits went unnoticed, except for muddy paw prints on the breakfast table.

It did not take long for other squirrels in the neighborhood to learn where the seeds and nuts were. Sometimes there was a bushy-tailed traffic jam on the feeder, but the moment Stormy appeared, she chased the others away. She ruled the feeder like a queen.

The Gillises became so much interested in their furry friends that they wanted to learn more about them. One evening Linda sat cross-legged on the living-room floor reading a book about squirrels that she had obtained from the public library. Mrs. Gillis sat in a chair reading the paper.

"Mother," Linda began, "it says here that a

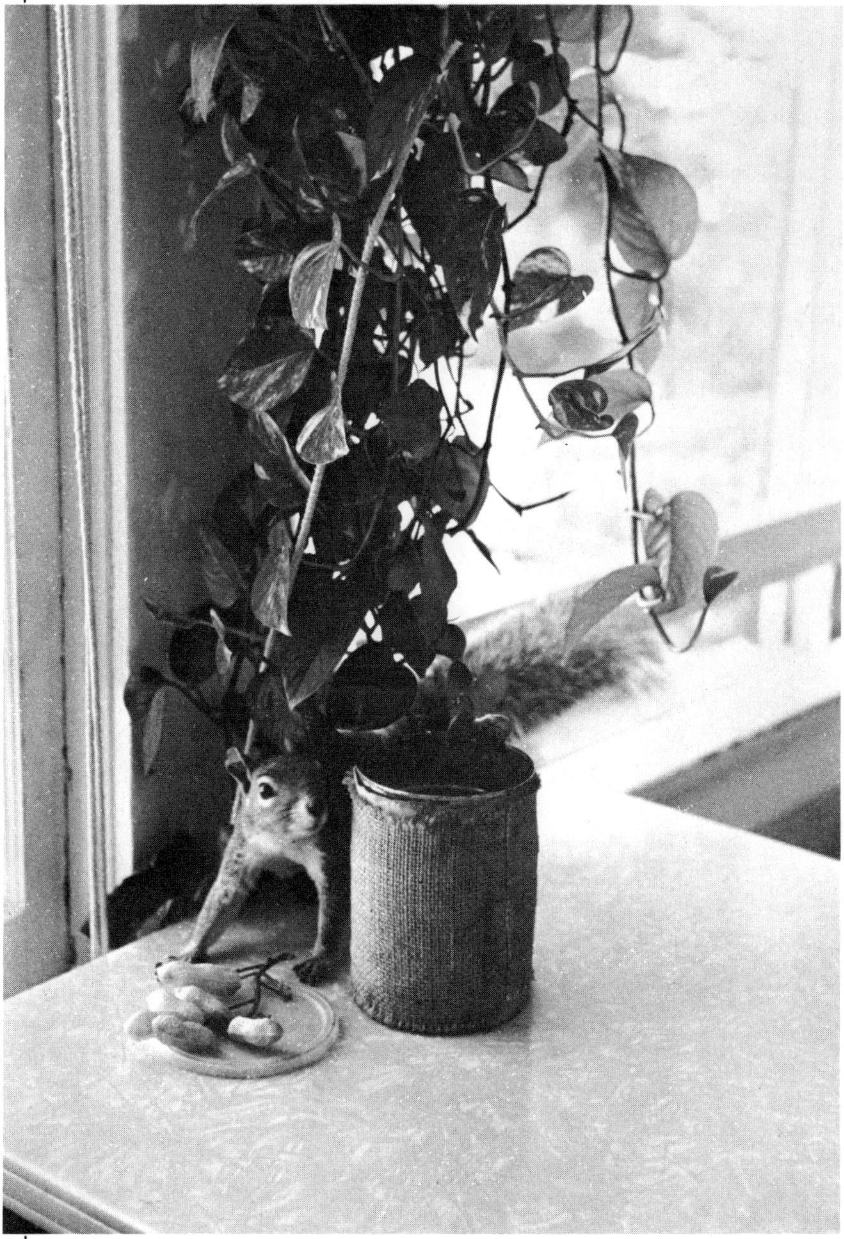

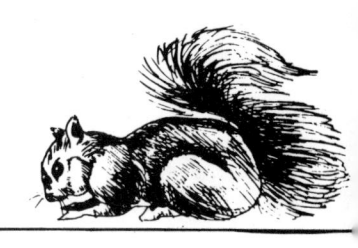

Stormy, THE SQUIRREL THAT CAME BACK

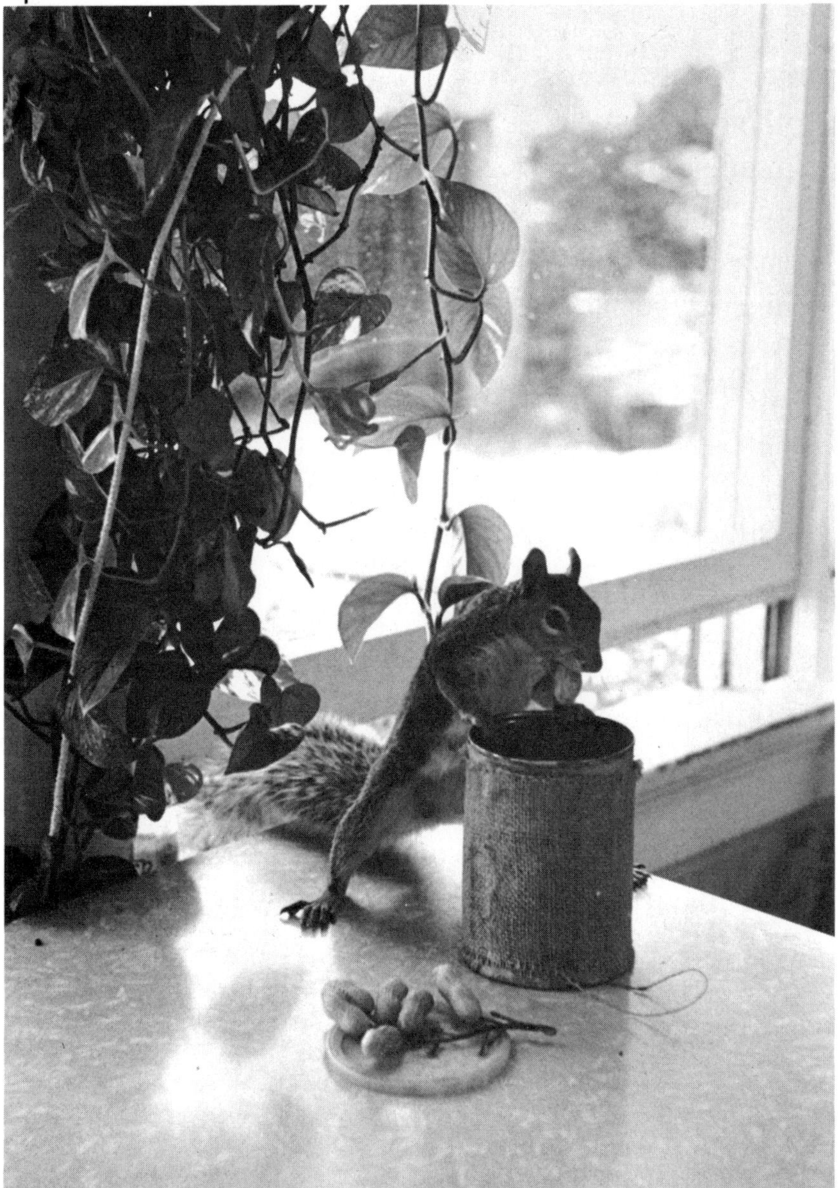

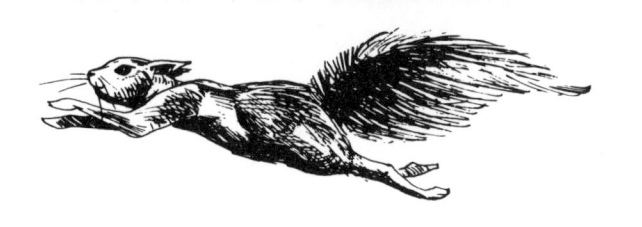

Stormy, THE SQUIRREL THAT CAME BACK

squirrel will bury from 4,000 to 5,000 nuts a year."

"I'm not surprised," her mother replied. "I've seen Stormy stuff three nuts into her mouth at one time. Then she'd go off and bury them, and a few minutes later she'd be back for more. Your father says that when he mows the yard, nuts fly all over the place. He thinks we could dig almost anywhere in the back yard and find a nut."

"According to this book," Linda continued, "squirrels have fairly good memories about where they've hidden the nuts. In the forest, it says, the acorns they do forget about make more oak trees. With more new trees, there will be more nuts for other squirrels to bury, and on and on it goes."

"It also says that squirrels have a good sense of smell. Even when there are several inches of snow on the ground, a squirrel will start to dig at one certain spot and always come up with a nut. Besides, the squirrels can tell ahead of time whether it is a good nut. Squirrels just don't dig up spoiled nuts. Isn't that amazing?"

"I, too, read something on squirrels the other day," Mrs. Gillis said. "Squirrels are supposed to be lazy, despite their being quick. They sleep a great deal in the daytime and stay in their nests in bad weather. Whatever expert wrote that item didn't know Stormy. That little girl isn't going to stay away from our feeder in order to sleep. She doesn't care about bad weather, either. The other day when it rained hard, she was on the feeder eating nuts. You never saw such a soggy-looking animal!"

The handouts that the Gillises continued to put on the feeder kept the squirrels coming almost all winter. Only in the coldest and iciest weather did they fail to appear. Traffic on the feeder continued to be heavy, but the family kept the window closed, except for the few seconds it took to put out the nuts and seeds.

Happy never lost interest in watching her play-

Stormy, THE SQUIRREL THAT CAME BACK

mates. She kept her wet nose pressed against the glass every day for hours at a time.

When the weather began to grow warm again, Linda started to watch the hollow-tree apartment.

After weeks had gone by and not one squirrel had appeared, she mentioned the fact to Jeff.

"Forget it," was Jeff's answer. "There's still plenty of time.

"I thought maybe they remembered what had happened last year when Stormy fell out of the apartment during the storm. That tree trunk does sway a lot when it gets real windy."

"Good grief, Linda," Jeff replied. "There are plenty of squirrels and plenty of hollow trees. Anyway, squirrels couldn't remember things like that."

One day Linda was sitting at the desk in her room doing her homework. She glanced outside.

Stormy, THE SQUIRREL THAT CAME BACK

Suddenly she jumped up and ran to the window. There, looking back at her from the hollow-tree apartment, was a gray squirrel.

"Come here, everybody," Linda called. "Spring is here! There's a squirrel in the apartment!"

As the family crowded at the window to watch, Mrs. Gillis remarked that there weren't any leafy decorations there this year.

"If that is Stormy," she remarked, "and I think it is, she isn't much of a housekeeper. There's hardly any leafy decoration in the hollow this year. Stormy's parents cared more than she does about adding greenery to the apartment."

No one else seemed to care, however, whether the apartment was decorated, as long as Stormy was back in her first home.

"Don't let's ever move from this house," Linda said. "Pretty soon we'll have Stormy's babies coming to the feeder, and next year there's sure to be another family in the apartment. I'll bet we're the squirreliest family in town."

"Speak for yourself, Linda," Jeff replied. "You may be squirrelly, but I'm a nut." Everyone laughed, and judging from the screeching noises outside, so did the squirrels.

About the Author

ELIZABETH GRAVES LUNT is a native of Kansas City, who began writing and taking photographs at the end of World War II. Following her marriage to William Lunt and the birth of their two daughters, Mrs. Lunt joined the staff of *The Kansas City Star* and subsequently began a successful career as a freelance photo-journalist. Her husband and their younger daughter and the family dog are among the characters pictured in the story of Stormy. The Lunts make their home in Kansas City, Missouri.